HOLIDAY HOUSE

MICHAEL HARDCASTLE

ERNEST BENN LIMITED

First published 1977 by Ernest Benn Limited
25 New Street Square, London EC4A 3JA
& Sovereign Way, Tonbridge, Kent TN9 1RW
Australia: TC Lothian Pty Limited, Melbourne
Canada: The General Publishing Company
Limited, Toronto
© Michael Hardcastle 1977
Illustrations © Ernest Benn Limited 1977

ISBN 0 510–07724–2

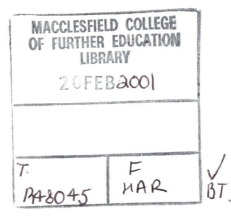
Printed in Great Britain by
William Clowes & Sons, Limited
London, Beccles and Colchester

HOLIDAY HOUSE

1

In the kitchen,
Mrs Bell was getting breakfast.
There was a good, warm smell
of eggs and bacon and fried bread.

Mrs Bell's holiday house
was called Sea View
and it was right on the front
at Rockport. Some of her guests
never went on holiday anywhere else.
"That smells good, Mum," said Steve,
putting his head round the door.
"Oh, Steve," Mrs Bell said.
"Could you tell Mr Smith it's ready?

Everyone else has come down."
"Okay, but I'm in a bit of a rush.
I've got a job to do
down by the harbour,
helping a bloke on his boat."
Mrs Bell nodded.

She knew that
Steve really enjoyed his job.
He worked on his own
at painting and building
and doing repairs.

Steve went upstairs
to Mr Smith's room.

Mr Smith had arrived at Sea View
in the middle of the week.
Most guests were couples;
husbands and wives, or families;
but Smith had arrived on his own.

Mrs Bell thought he had friends
in Rockport.
All the same, he didn't act as if
he was on holiday.

The door of Mr Smith's room was
open, but Steve knocked and waited.
There was no answer,
so Steve walked in.
To his surprise, he saw
that the bed was neatly made up.
It didn't look as though
it had been slept in.

Steve looked round the room
and saw two suitcases
on top of the wardrobe.
That was a good sign.

It meant that Smith hadn't left
without paying the bill.
There were always some people
who did tricks like that.
Perhaps Smith had just gone out
for a walk.

Steve gave his mother the news.
As he set off for the harbour
he wondered why a man on his own
needed two suitcases.

He had just turned onto the Prom,
when he spotted Anna, his girlfriend.
His heart always jumped
when he saw her;
she was the prettiest girl
he'd ever known.

They had first met
only a couple of weeks ago,
when there was a big fire on the pier.
Anna always told people now
that Steve had saved her life.
In a way, that was true.

She swung round at once
and her eyes lighted up.
"Steve! Hey, great to see you."

12

She put her arms round him
and they kissed.
It didn't matter at all
that several people stopped
to stare at them.
Holidaymakers would stop
to watch anything.
"I'm just going to see about
getting a job at the disco,"
Anna told him.

She had worked on the pier,
  but the fire had put an end to that.
  Steve told her about Mr Smith.
"You," laughed Anna.
"It's all in your mind.
  This poor man sounds okay.
  Just a bit odd, that's all."

"Maybe you're right," Steve said.
"Look Anna, I'll have to go now.
  I'm working on Jack Edgar's boat,
  but I'll see you tonight, okay?"

14

"Okay, Steve.
  Keep your fingers crossed for me."
She smiled and waved goodbye.

2

Jack Edgar was already at work
on his boat, *Lady Love*,
when Steve reached the harbour.
"Glad to see you," he called to Steve.
"I need some help."
Steve climbed up onto the deck.
He took his shirt off.

If the weather stayed like this,
he would soon be as brown as Anna.
Steve thought about her
as he worked on the roof of the cabin.
He hoped she would get the job;
Anna hated to have nothing to do.

It was midday
when Steve suddenly heard Jack
talking to someone.
"I'm sorry, but I can't take you out
   tonight," Jack was saying.
"But you can have the money in cash,"
   the other man replied.

17

"Half of it now, and the other half
   when we get back.
   Just one trip, that's all.
   I'm offering a lot of money, you know."
"Mm, I'd like to, but I can't —
   not tonight, anyway," Jack said.

"It must be tonight," was the reply.
"Do you know anyone else I could try?
   I need to fix up something quick,
   you see."

By now, Steve was really interested.
Slowly he moved
so that he could see the man
who was talking to Jack.
Then he got a shock.
He knew the man.
It was Smith!

"You could try Freddy Wilson,"
Jack was telling him.
"His boat's always ready to go out."
Smith waved his thanks and left.

Steve was sure he hadn't noticed him.
He was glad about that.
"What was all that about, then?"
Steve asked.
Jack picked up a paintbrush.

20

"Oh, some bloke who said
   he wanted to go out
   for a bit of sea fishing tonight.
   Offered me plenty of money to do it."

"Do you know him?" Steve asked.
   Jack shook his head.
"I've seen him about.
   But he's not local, I'm sure of that.
   I don't think he knows much about
   fishing. But he's up to something.
   Something fishy."
   He stopped, and then laughed.
"Hey, that's not bad,
   is it Steve? Fishy business,
   not fishing business!"

Steve smiled,
   but he was thinking of something else.

Smith had two suitcases in his room.
So perhaps he was planning to leave
without telling anyone
— to get out of the country
without a passport.

If that was it,
he would need to have all his things
with him. That would explain
why he had two suitcases.
He wasn't really on holiday at all.

22

"Do you think Freddy Wilson
  will take him out, then?" Steve asked.
"I expect so," Jack replied.
"Freddy doesn't miss a chance
  of making some spare cash.
  He's got a good boat, too.
  And this bloke wants to go out
  right into the Channel."

For the next few minutes
Steve got on with his work.
But he couldn't stop thinking
about Smith and the fishing trip.
At last,
he threw down his paintbrush
and told Jack he'd be back
in half an hour.

3

At that time of day,
Sea View Guest House was empty,
apart from Steve's mother.
Steve went straight upstairs
and knocked on Smith's door.
As he'd expected,
there was no reply.
Steve went in.
His heart was thumping a bit.

He didn't like going into
a guest's room,
but he had to find out
what Smith was up to.

If Smith was planning to leave
the country, Steve was going to make
sure he paid his bill before he went.
His mother couldn't afford
to lose the money.
Carefully, Steve lifted down
the first suitcase, which wasn't
as heavy as he'd expected.

It wasn't locked either.
When he lifted the lid,
he saw that it contained
only a few clothes.

The second case contained even less;
it was empty, except for
a handful of small, see-through bags —
the sort of bags used for sandwiches
and other food.

Then Steve checked the wardrobe.
Not much in there, either.
So it didn't look
as though Smith was planning
to leave the country, after all.

28

But Steve was still puzzled.
Why did Smith have so little to put
in those suitcases?
"Maybe Anna's right," he thought.
"Perhaps Smith is just a bit odd."

But when he went down
to the kitchen, he asked his mother
how long Smith was staying.

"He's booked in for the week,"
Mrs Bell replied.
"But a funny thing happened
this morning. I went out
into the hall and he was
on the telephone.
I couldn't help hearing what he said.
He said something like: 'Yes, tonight.
One more day here will drive
me crazy'.

Then when he saw me,
he stopped talking.
I hope he didn't mean Sea View."
She looked upset.

Steve almost told his mother
about the suitcases.
But he didn't.
She would have been mad if she knew
he had been in a guest's room.
So, he gave her a quick hug
and said, "Don't worry, Mum."
And went back to the harbour.

That evening, he wasn't surprised
when his mother said
that Mr Smith had gone out
fishing. He ate his meal fast.
Then he went into town to meet Anna.
As soon as he saw her
he knew that she hadn't got the job
at the disco. She looked so sad.

"Hey, cheer up!" he said,
  taking her in his arms
  and kissing her.

"All the drinks are on me, tonight.
  You'll get the next job you go for,
  I know it."
  Soon Anna began to cheer up.
  She told Steve about the disco
  and the other girls she'd met there.

Then she added,
"We had plenty of time to talk
and Maria — that's one of the girls —
told me something about your Mr Smith.

Seems like you were right.
He *is* up to something.
He went to the disco last night
with a friend of his. A big bloke.
Looked more like a body guard
than a friend. No one liked them.
The boss of the disco
didn't trust them either.
He told them to go."
Anna stopped. She looked serious.

"Maria thinks they are trying
to push drugs. But not
at the disco. They wouldn't dare.

34

She also said that as they left,
Smith said something like,
'I'll get the stuff tomorrow and
then we can clear out of this place.'
She didn't know what he meant."

Steve told her about
Smith's fishing trip. He went on,
"I've been thinking.
He must pick up the stuff
when he goes out fishing.
Stuff like that must be coming
into the country on a ship.

Smith must have found some way
of getting hold of it
before the ship gets into port."
"Steve," said Anna,
"What do you think we should do?"

"First, we'll check
if Freddy Wilson is back yet.
Then I must go up to Sea View."
He sounded worried.
"Smith could be dangerous."
Anna nodded.

36

"Look," Steve went on,
"Could you ring the police
 and get them there?
 Tell them anything. But get them."
Anna kissed him
and went off into the darkness.

4

When Steve reached Sea View,
the house was almost in darkness.
Only one light was showing.
It was in Smith's room.

Then, while he was still
looking up at the window,
the light went out.
"Well, that's okay," Steve thought.
"Smith's back
and now he's ready for bed.
I'd better wait here for the police."
Suddenly, everything
happened at once.

Just as Anna arrived at the gate,
the front door opened.
Steve found himself face to face
with Mr Smith!

Each was as surprised as the other.
For a moment, no one moved.
Then Smith charged forward,
pushing his way between Steve
and Anna.

He was carrying a suitcase
in each hand, and one of them
banged into Anna.
The blow was hard enough
to knock her over.

Steve was making a grab at Smith
when he saw Anna fall.
He paused —
and Smith dashed down the path.

40

Anna saw what was happening.
"I'm okay," she yelled.
"Get after him, Steve!"
By now, Smith was running as fast
as he could towards the town centre.

But the two cases
were slowing him down.
Steve soon began to catch up.
But Smith wasn't going
to let himself be caught
if he could help it.

Suddenly he stopped,
swung round —
and threw one of the cases at Steve.
Steve tried to jump
out of the way,
but the case hit his legs —
and he fell.

The case burst open,
and packets of white powder
poured out like letters
from a postman's bag.

As Steve stared at them
in astonishment, a car
came racing down the Prom.
A blue light was flashing
on its roof.

"Well done, lad," the police driver
  said to Steve as he and his mate
  grabbed hold of Smith.
"You're Steve Bell, aren't you?"
  Steve was too out of breath
  to say a word. He just nodded.

"Your girlfriend rang us
  a few minutes ago," the driver said.
"We've known about Smith
  for some time.
  But we wanted to catch him
  with the stuff on him.

It's lucky for us
that you notice what's going on
around you."
Anna came up.
She put her arm round Steve,
and he grinned.
"Yes, I suppose I do!"

INNER RING HIPSTERS

RED CIRCLE HIPSTERS

by Richard Parker

DIGGING FOR TREASURE
THE SUNDAY PAPERS
FLOOD
SAUSAGES ON THE SHORE

Four stories about Stringer, Dave,
Linda and Mag, who live in a southern
riverport town. You can find out
how they dig for treasure,
manage a paper round
and the strange adventure
of their picnic by the river.

GREEN CIRCLE HIPSTERS
by Clive King

HIGH JACKS, LOW JACKS
FIRST DAY OUT
THE ACCIDENT
THE SECRET

Four stories about Rima, a young
Asian girl and her brother Sami,
who are starting a new life
in England.

by Michael Hardcastle

FIRE ON THE SEA
CRASH CAR
HOLIDAY HOUSE
STRONG ARM

Steve and Anna live in Rockport, a
seaside town.
Read about their friends and what
they do; how they find a new sport—
stock car racing, and what happens
when there is a fire on the pier.